This book belongs to:

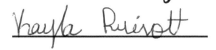

This book is dedicated to magical creatures everywhere.

Published in 2019 by Flowered Press
Copyright 2019 by Hayley Rose

Text and design by Hayley Rose
Illustrations by Lynx Animation Studios

ISBN: 978-0-9998073-1-6
Library of Congress Cataloging-in-Publication Process

Printed in China

The Thankful Unicorn:

Release Your Inner Magic

By Hayley Rose
Illustrated by Lynx Animation Studios

Date _____

Today I am thankful for:

1. _____
2. _____
3. _____

My dreams and goals:

1. _____
2. _____
3. _____

What I love about myself:

1. _____
2. _____
3. _____

My affirmations:

1. _____
2. _____
3. _____

"Live by what truly makes you happy." ~ The Thankful Unicorn

Date _____

Today I am thankful for:

1. _____
2. _____
3. _____

My dreams and goals:

1. _____
2. _____
3. _____

What I love about myself:

1. _____
2. _____
3. _____

My affirmations:

1. _____
2. _____
3. _____

"There is only one way to happiness and that is to cease worrying about things which are beyond the power of our will." ~ Epictetus

Date _____

Today I am thankful for:

1. _____
2. _____
3. _____

My dreams and goals:

1. _____
2. _____
3. _____

What I love about myself:

1. _____
2. _____
3. _____

My affirmations:

1. _____
2. _____
3. _____

"Let us be grateful to people who make us happy, they are the charming gardeners who make our souls blossom." ~ Marcel Proust

Date _____

Today I am thankful for:

1. _____

2. _____

3. _____

My dreams and goals:

1. _____

2. _____

3. _____

What I love about myself:

1. _____

2. _____

3. _____

My affirmations:

1. _____

2. _____

3. _____

"The direction of the mind is more important than its progress." ~ Joseph Jonbert

Date _____

Today I am thankful for:

1. _____
2. _____
3. _____

My dreams and goals:

1. _____
2. _____
3. _____

What I love about myself:

1. _____
2. _____
3. _____

My affirmations:

1. _____
2. _____
3. _____

"Happiness is a habit - cultivate it." ~ Elbert Hubbard

Date _____

Today I am thankful for:

1. _____
2. _____
3. _____

My dreams and goals:

1. _____
2. _____
3. _____

What I love about myself:

1. _____
2. _____
3. _____

My affirmations:

1. _____
2. _____
3. _____

"Gratitude is the fairest blossom which springs from the soul."
~ Henry Ward Beecher

Date _____

Today I am thankful for:

1. _____
2. _____
3. _____

My dreams and goals:

1. _____
2. _____
3. _____

What I love about myself:

1. _____
2. _____
3. _____

My affirmations:

1. _____
2. _____
3. _____

"Calmness of mind is one of the beautiful jewels of wisdom." ~ James Allen

Date _____

▷▷▷▷▷ ➤ ≫ • ≪ ◄ ◄◄◄◄ ◎ ▷▷▷▷ ➤ ≫ • ≪ ◄ ◄◄◄◄

Today I am thankful for:

1. _____

2. _____

3. _____

▷▷▷▷▷ ➤ ≫ • ≪ ◄ ◄◄◄◄ ◎ ▷▷▷▷ ➤ ≫ • ≪ ◄ ◄◄◄◄

▷▷▷▷▷ ➤ ≫ • ≪ ◄ ◄◄◄◄ 🦄 ▷▷▷▷ ➤ ≫ • ≪ ◄ ◄◄◄◄

My dreams and goals:

1. _____

2. _____

3. _____

▷▷▷▷▷ ➤ ≫ • ≪ ◄ ◄◄◄◄ ◎ ▷▷▷▷ ➤ ≫ • ≪ ◄ ◄◄◄◄

▷▷▷▷▷ ➤ ≫ • ≪ ◄ ◄◄◄◄ ☆ ▷▷▷▷ ➤ ≫ • ≪ ◄ ◄◄◄◄

What I love about myself:

1. _____

2. _____

3. _____

▷▷▷▷▷ ➤ ≫ • ≪ ◄ ◄◄◄◄ ◎ ▷▷▷▷ ➤ ≫ • ≪ ◄ ◄◄◄◄

▷▷▷▷▷ ➤ ≫ • ≪ ◄ ◄◄◄◄ 🌷 ▷▷▷▷ ➤ ≫ • ≪ ◄ ◄◄◄◄

My affirmations:

1. _____

2. _____

3. _____

▷▷▷▷▷ ➤ ≫ • ≪ ◄ ◄◄◄◄ ◎ ▷▷▷▷ ➤ ≫ • ≪ ◄ ◄◄◄◄

"Wonder is the desire for knowledge." ~ Thomas Aquinas

Date _____

Today I am thankful for:

1. _____
2. _____
3. _____

My dreams and goals:

1. _____
2. _____
3. _____

What I love about myself:

1. _____
2. _____
3. _____

My affirmations:

1. _____
2. _____
3. _____

"Our life is what our thoughts make it." ~ James Allen

Date _____

Today I am thankful for:

1. _____
2. _____
3. _____

My dreams and goals:

1. _____
2. _____
3. _____

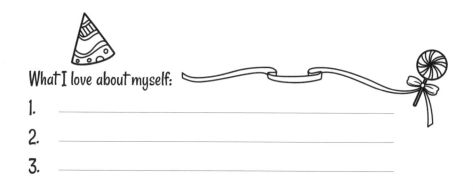

What I love about myself:

1. _____
2. _____
3. _____

My affirmations:

1. _____
2. _____
3. _____

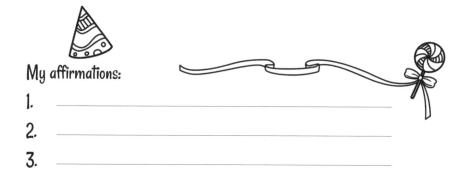

"Choose to be positive. Choose to be thankful. You are a direct result of your thoughts." ~ The Thankful Unicorn

Date _____

Today I am thankful for:

1. _____
2. _____
3. _____

My dreams and goals:

1. _____
2. _____
3. _____

What I love about myself:

1. _____
2. _____
3. _____

My affirmations:

1. _____
2. _____
3. _____

"Attach yourself to what is spiritually superior, regardless of what other people think or do. Hold to your true aspirations no matter what is going on around you." ~ Epictetus

Date _____

Today I am thankful for:

1. _____
2. _____
3. _____

My dreams and goals:

1. _____
2. _____
3. _____

What I love about myself:

1. _____
2. _____
3. _____

My affirmations:

1. _____
2. _____
3. _____

"What you think, so shall you be." ~ The Thankful Unicorn

Date _____

Today I am thankful for:

1. _____
2. _____
3. _____

My dreams and goals:

1. _____
2. _____
3. _____

What I love about myself:

1. _____
2. _____
3. _____

My affirmations:

1. _____
2. _____
3. _____

"Happiness resides not in possessions, and not in gold, happy dwells in the soul."
~ Democritus

Today I am thankful for:

1. _____
2. _____
3. _____

My dreams and goals:

1. _____
2. _____
3. _____

What I love about myself:

1. _____
2. _____
3. _____

My affirmations:

1. _____
2. _____
3. _____

"Dwell in a place of gratitude and you will always be home."
~ The Thankful Unicorn

Date _____

Today I am thankful for:

1. _____
2. _____
3. _____

My dreams and goals:

1. _____
2. _____
3. _____

What I love about myself:

1. _____
2. _____
3. _____

My affirmations:

1. _____
2. _____
3. _____

"The essence of all beautiful art, all great art, is gratitude." ~ Friedrich Nietzsche

Date _____

Today I am thankful for:

1. _____
2. _____
3. _____

My dreams and goals:

1. _____
2. _____
3. _____

What I love about myself:

1. _____
2. _____
3. _____

My affirmations:

1. _____
2. _____
3. _____

"No duty is more urgent than that of returning thanks." ~ James Allen

Date _____

Today I am thankful for:

1. _____
2. _____
3. _____

My dreams and goals:

1. _____
2. _____
3. _____

What I love about myself:

1. _____
2. _____
3. _____

My affirmations:

1. _____
2. _____
3. _____

"Live with a thankful heart, and you will always feel loved." ~ The Thankful Unicorn

Date _____

Today I am thankful for:

1. _____

2. _____

3. _____

My dreams and goals:

1. _____

2. _____

3. _____

What I love about myself:

1. _____

2. _____

3. _____

My affirmations:

1. _____

2. _____

3. _____

"Dream lofty dreams, and as you dream, so you shall become, your vision
is the promise of what you shall one day be." ~ James Allen

Date _____

Today I am thankful for:

1. _____
2. _____
3. _____

My dreams and goals:

1. _____
2. _____
3. _____

What I love about myself:

1. _____
2. _____
3. _____

My affirmations:

1. _____
2. _____
3. _____

"When life gives you lemons, make lemonade." ~ Elbert Hubbard

Date _____

Today I am thankful for:

1. _____

2. _____

3. _____

My dreams and goals:

1. _____

2. _____

3. _____

What I love about myself:

1. _____

2. _____

3. _____

My affirmations:

1. _____

2. _____

3. _____

"Be Happy. Live Thankful." ~ The Thankful Unicorn

Date _____

Today I am thankful for:

1. _____
2. _____
3. _____

My dreams and goals:

1. _____
2. _____
3. _____

What I love about myself:

1. _____
2. _____
3. _____

My affirmations:

1. _____
2. _____
3. _____

"Live by what truly makes you happy." ~ The Thankful Unicorn

Date _____

Today I am thankful for:

1. _____

2. _____

3. _____

My dreams and goals:

1. _____

2. _____

3. _____

What I love about myself:

1. _____

2. _____

3. _____

My affirmations:

1. _____

2. _____

3. _____

"There is only one way to happiness and that is to cease worrying about things which are beyond the power of our will." ~ Epictetus

Date _____

Today I am thankful for:

1. _____
2. _____
3. _____

My dreams and goals:

1. _____
2. _____
3. _____

What I love about myself:

1. _____
2. _____
3. _____

My affirmations:

1. _____
2. _____
3. _____

"Let us be grateful to people who make us happy, they are the charming gardeners who make our souls blossom." ~ Marcel Proust

Date _____

Today I am thankful for:

1. _____
2. _____
3. _____

My dreams and goals:

1. _____
2. _____
3. _____

What I love about myself:

1. _____
2. _____
3. _____

My affirmations:

1. _____
2. _____
3. _____

"The direction of the mind is more important than its progress." ~ Joseph Jonbert

Date _____

Today I am thankful for:

1. _____
2. _____
3. _____

My dreams and goals:

1. _____
2. _____
3. _____

What I love about myself:

1. _____
2. _____
3. _____

My affirmations:

1. _____
2. _____
3. _____

"Happiness is a habit - cultivate it." ~ Elbert Hubbard

Date _____

Today I am thankful for:

1. _____
2. _____
3. _____

My dreams and goals:

1. _____
2. _____
3. _____

What I love about myself:

1. _____
2. _____
3. _____

My affirmations:

1. _____
2. _____
3. _____

"Gratitude is the fairest blossom which springs from the soul."
~ Henry Ward Beecher

Date _____

Today I am thankful for:

1. _____
2. _____
3. _____

My dreams and goals:

1. _____
2. _____
3. _____

What I love about myself:

1. _____
2. _____
3. _____

My affirmations:

1. _____
2. _____
3. _____

"Calmness of mind is one of the beautiful jewels of wisdom." ~ James Allen

Date _____

Today I am thankful for:

1. _____
2. _____
3. _____

My dreams and goals:

1. _____
2. _____
3. _____

What I love about myself:

1. _____
2. _____
3. _____

My affirmations:

1. _____
2. _____
3. _____

"Wonder is the desire for knowledge." ~ Thomas Aquinas

Today I am thankful for:

1. _____
2. _____
3. _____

My dreams and goals:

1. _____
2. _____
3. _____

What I love about myself:

1. _____
2. _____
3. _____

My affirmations:

1. _____
2. _____
3. _____

"Our life is what our thoughts make it." ~ James Allen

Today I am thankful for:

1. _____

2. _____

3. _____

My dreams and goals:

1. _____

2. _____

3. _____

What I love about myself:

1. _____

2. _____

3. _____

My affirmations:

1. _____

2. _____

3. _____

"Choose to be positive. Choose to be thankful. You are a direct result of your thoughts." ~ The Thankful Unicorn

Date _____

Today I am thankful for:

1. _____
2. _____
3. _____

My dreams and goals:

1. _____
2. _____
3. _____

What I love about myself:

1. _____
2. _____
3. _____

My affirmations:

1. _____
2. _____
3. _____

"Attach yourself to what is spiritually superior, regardless of what other people think or do.
Hold to your true aspirations no matter what is going on around you." ~ Epictetus